If Lost, Please Return To:

_____

For God so loved the world that he gave his one and only Son, that whoever believes in him shall not perish but have eternal life.
    John 3:16

"For I know the plans I have for you," declares the Lord, "plans to prosper you and not to harm you, plans to give you hope and a future."

Jeremiah 29:11

And we know that in all things God works for the good of those who love him, who have been called according to his purpose.

Romans 8:28

I can do all things through Him who gives me strength.
Philippians 4:13

In the beginning, God created the heavens and the earth.
Genesis 1:1

Trust in the Lord with all your heart and lean not on your own understanding.

Proverbs 3:5

In all your ways acknowledge Him, and He will make your paths straight.
Proverbs 3:6

Do not conform any longer to the patterns of this world, but be transformed by the renewing of your mind. Then you will be able to test and approve what God's will is-his good, pleasing, and perfect will.

Romans 12:2

Do not be anxious about anything, but in everything, by prayer and petition, with thanksgiving, present your requests to God.
Philippians 4:6

Therefore go and make disciples of all nations, baptizing them in the name of the Father and of the Son and of the Holy Spirit.
Matthew 28:19

For it is by grace you have been saved, through faith-and this not from yourselves, it is the gift of God-
Ephesians 2:8

> But the fruit of the Spirit is love, joy, peace, patience, kindness, faithfulness.
> Galatians 5:22

Therefore, I urge you, brothers, in view of God's mercy, to offer your bodies as living sacrifices, holy and pleasing to God-this is your spiritual act of worship.
Romans 12:1

> The thief comes only to steal and kill and destroy; I have come that they may have life, and have it to the full.
> John 10:10

For I am with you, and no one is going to attack and harm you, because I have many people in this city.
Acts 18:10

One night the Lord spoke to Paul in a vision: "Do not be afraid; keep on speaking, do not be silent."
Acts 18:9

So Paul stayed for a year and a half, teaching them the word of God.
Acts 18:11

I have been crucified with Christ and I no longer live, but Christ lives in me. The life I live in the body, I live by faith in the Son of God, who loved me and gave himself for me.
Galatians 2:20

If we confess our sins, he is faithful and just and will forgive us our sins and purify us from all unrighteousness.
1 John 1:19

For all have sinned and fall short of the glory of God.
Romans 3:23

Jesus answered, "I am the way and the truth and the life. No one comes to the Father except through me.
John 14:6

And teaching them to obey everything I have commanded you. And surely I am with you always, to the very end of the age.

Matthew 28:20

But God demonstrates his own love for us in this: While we were still sinners, Christ died for us.
Romans 5:8

Finally, brothers, whatever is true, whatever is noble, whatever is right, whatever is pure, whatever is lovely, whatever is admirable-if anything is excellent or praiseworthy-think about such things.

Philippians 4:8

And the peace of God, which transcends all understanding, will guard your hearts and your minds in Christ Jesus.
Philippians 4:7

Have I not commanded you? Be strong and courageous. Do not be terrified; do not be discouraged, for the Lord your God will be with you wherever you go.
Joshua 1:9

But those who hope in the Lord will renew their strength. They will soar on wings like eagles; they will run and not grow weary, they will walk and not be faint.
Isaiah 40:31

Not by works, so that no one can boast
Ephesians 2:9

For the wages of sin is death, but the gift of God is eternal life in Christ Jesus our Lord.
Romans 6:23

Gentleness and self-control. Against such things there is no law.
Galatians 5:23

But he was pierced for our transgressions, he was crushed for our iniquities; the punishment that brought us peace was upon him, and by his wounds we are healed.
Isaiah 53:5

But in your hearts set apart Christ as Lord. Always be prepared to give an answer to everyone who asks you to give the reason for the hope that you have. But do this with gentleness and respect.

1 Peter 3:15

All scripture is God-breathed and is useful for teaching, rebuking, correcting and training in righteousness.
2 Timothy 3:16

> But seek first his kingdom and his righteousness, and all these things will be given to you as well.
> Matthew 6:33

Let us fix our eyes on Jesus, the author and perfecter of our faith, who for the joy set before him endured the cross, scoring its shame, and sat down at the right hand of the throne of God.
Hebrews 12:2

Cast all your anxiety on him because he cares for you.

1 Peter 5:7

For we are God's workmanship, created in Chris Jesus to do good works, which God prepared in advance for us to do.
Ephesians 2:10

No temptation has seized you except what is common to man. And God is faithful; he will not let you be tempted beyond what you can bear. But when you are tempted, he will also provide a way out so that you can stand up under it.
1 Corinthians 10:13

"Come to me, all you who are weary and burdened, and I will give you rest."
Matthew 11:28

Now faith is being sure of what we hope for and certain of what we do not see.
Hebrews 11:1

Therefore, if anyone is in Christ, he is a new creation; the old has gone, the new has come!
2 Corinthians 5:17

Keep your lives free from the love of money and be content with what you have, because God has said, "Never will I leave you; never will I forsake you."
Hebrews 13:5

But he said to me, "My grace is sufficient for you, for my power is made perfect in weakness." Therefore I will boast all the more gladly about my weaknesses, so that Christ's power may rest on me.
2 Corinthians 12:9

That if you confess with your mouth, "Jesus is Lord," and believe in your heart that God raised him from the dead, you will be saved.
Romans 10:9

So do not fear, for I am with you; do not be dismayed, for I am your God. I will strengthen and help you; I will uphold you with my righteous right hand.
Isaiah 41:10

The God said, "Let us make in our image, in our likeness, and let them rule over the fish of the sea and the birds of the air, over the livestock, over all the earth, and over all the creatures that move along the ground."

Genesis 1:26

Take my yoke upon you and learn from me, for I am gentle and humble in heart, and you will find rest for your souls.
Matthew 11:29

"I have told you these things, so that in me you may have peace. In this would you will have trouble. But take heart! I have overcome the world."
John 16:33

But you will receive power when the Holy Spirit comes on you; and you will be my witnesses in Jerusalem, and in all Judea and Samaria, and to the ends of the earth.
Acts 1:8

For God did not give us a spirit of timidity, but a spirit of power, of love and of self-discipline.

2 Timothy 1:7

Surely he took up our infirmities and carried our sorrows, yet we considered him stricken by God, smitten by him, and afflicted.
Isaiah 53:4

God made him who had no sin to be sin for us, so that in him we might become the righteousness of God.
2 Corinthians 5:21

May the God of hope fill you with all joy and peace as you trust in him, so that you may overflow with hope by the power of the Holy Spirit.
Romans 15:13

Jesus said to her, "I am the resurrection and the life. He who believes in me will live, even though he dies."
John 11:25

And without faith it is impossible to please God, because anyone who comes to him must believe that he exists and that he rewards those who earnestly seek him.
Hebrews 11:6

"I tell you the truth, whoever hears my word and believes him who sent me has eternal live and will not be condemned; he has crossed over from death to life."
John 5:24

Consider it pure joy, my brothers, whenever you face trials of many kinds.

James 1:2

We all, like sheep, have gone astray, each of us has turned on his own way; and the Lord has laid on him the iniquity of us all.
Isaiah 53:6

Peter replied, "Repent and be baptized, every one of you, in the name of Jesus Christ for the forgiveness of your sins. And you will receive the gift of the Holy Spirit."

Acts 2:38

Now to him who is able to do immeasurably more than all we ask or imagine, according to his power that is at work within us.
Ephesians 3:20

For my yoke is easy and my burden is light.
Matthew 11:30

So God created man in his own image, in the image of God he created him; male and female he created them.
Genesis 1:27

> Therefore, as God's chosen people, holy and dearly loved, clothe yourselves with compassion, kindness, humility, gentleness and patience.
> Colossians 3:12

Therefore, confess your sins to each other and pray for each other so that you may be healed. The prayer of a righteous man is powerful and effective.

James 5:16

> And my God will meet all your needs according to his glorious riches in Christ Jesus.
> Philippians 4:19

In the beginning was the Word, and the Word was with God, and the Word was God.
John 1:1

Do you not know that your body is a temple of the Holy Spirit, who is in you, whom you have received from God? You are not your own.
1 Corinthians 6:19

This is how we know what love is: Jesus Christ laid down his life for us. And we ought to lay down our lives for our brothers.
1 John 3:16

> How good and pleasant it is when brothers live together in unity!
> Psalms 133:1

Peace I leave with you; my peace I give you. I do not give to you as the world gives. Do not let your hearts be troubled and do not be afraid.
John 14:27

> Greater love has no one than this, that he lay down his life for his friends.
> John 15:13

He showed you, O Man, what is good. And what does the Lord require of you? To act just and to love mercy and to walk humbly with your god.
Micah 6:8

Consequently, faith comes from hearing the message, and the message is heard through the word of Christ.
Romans 10:17

Yet to all who received him, to those who believed in his name, he gave the right to become children of God.
John 1:12

> Blessed is the man who perseveres under trial, because when he has stood the test, he will receive the crown of life that God has promised to those who love him.
> James 1:12

Because you know that the testing of your faith develops perseverance.
James 1:3

Let us not give up meeting together, as some are in the habit of doing, but let us encourage one another—and all the more as you see the Day approaching.
Hebrews 10:25

Being confident of this, that he who began a good work in you will carry it on to completion until the day of Christ Jesus.
Philippians 1:16

Let us then approach the throne of grace with confidence, so that we may receive mercy and find grace to help us in our time of need.

Hebrews 4:16

Delight yourself in the Lord and he will give you the desires of your heart.
Psalms 37:4

For God did not send his Son into the world to condemn the world, but to save the world through him.

John 3:17

Salvation is found in no one else, for there is no other name under heaven given to men by which we must be saved.
Acts 4:12

You will keep in perfect peace him whose mind is steadfast, because he trusts you.
Isaiah 26:3

He himself bore our sins in his body on the tree, so that we might die to sins and live for righteousness; by his wounds you have been healed.
1 Peter 2:24

Then Jesus came to them and said, "All authority in heaven and on earth has been given to me."

Matthew 28:18

Whatever you do, work at it with all your heart, as working for the lord, not for men.
Colossians 3:23

Jesus replied, "Love the Lord your God with all your heart and with all your soul and with all your mind."
Matthew 22:37

In the same way, let your light shine before men, that they may see you good deeds and praise your Father in heaven.
Matthew 5:16

"For my thoughts are not your thoughts, neither are your ways my ways," declares the Lord.
Isaiah 55:8

www.ingramcontent.com/pod-product-compliance
Lightning Source LLC
Chambersburg PA
CBHW070122110526
44587CB00017BA/3242